KOANS

The Lessons of Zen

Edited by Manuela Dunn Mascetti
Introduction by T. H. Barrett

NEW YORK

For information address:
Hyperion, 114 Fifth Avenue, New York, NY 10011

ISBN 0-7868-6252-1

Designed by Gautier Design, London
Image selection by Timeless Enterprise (UK) Ltd., London

Library of Congress Cataloging-in-Publication Data
Koans the lessons of Zen / edited by Manuela Dunn; introduction by T.H. Barrett. — [1st ed.]
    p.   cm.
    "Selections from . . . the Gateless gate (Mumonkan) and the Blue cliff records
(Hekiganroku)"—Pref.
    ISBN 0-7868-6252-1
    1. Koan. 2. Hui-k'ai, 1183-1260. Wu-men kuan.3. Yüan-wu, 1063-1135. Pi yen lu.
I. Dunn, Manuela, 1965– . II. Hui-k'ai, 1183-1260. Wu-men kuan. English. Selections.
III. Yüan-wu, 1063-1135. Pi yen lu. English. Selections.
BQ9289.5.K63 1996
294.3'443—dc20   96–33724
                                                                                      CIP

Printed and bound in the United States of America by Quebecor-Kingsport
FIRST EDITION
10 9 8 7 6 5 4 3 2 1

CONTENTS

INTRODUCTION

Now that the sound of "one hand clapping" has reverberated around our multicultural world, many people who have never undertaken Zen training have at least some idea of what a koan is. If asked, they would probably come up with a reasonable working definition, something like "a Zen riddle that defies logic," perhaps with a comment on the seemingly bizarre phrasing involved. Actually, the literal meaning of the word "koan" is somewhat unexpected: it signifies "a court case," or more concretely, "a file of legal documents." The very same word is even found in the titles of traditional Chinese detective stories, where, paradoxically, a puzzle-solving that is far from illogical is usually part of the plot.

But we must go back even further and consider the original context of the term. From the time of China's first emperor her rulers have administered the law through a bureaucratic hierarchy. A law court was a place of dread, and hell itself was popularly understood as another court of law writ large in the afterlife. To close the file of documents on a case, then, was not merely to solve a puzzle, but to resolve a matter of life and death—as much for the mandarin, with his superiors ready to scrutinize his every judgment, as for the poor unfortunates caught up in the legal process. What better word, then, for the documentation set before students of Zen, drawn from the words of earlier

enlightened masters? For how were such cases to be closed? There is no form of answer—verbal or nonverbal—that can possibly set aside such cases; the only possible form of closure is some form of enlightenment itself. We speak therefore of the study of koans as a system of education that would be shut down immediately by government inspectors in today's world: no curriculum; no time limit; above all, no success guaranteed, even to the committed and the intelligent.

True the Japanese Zen tradition has delimited a sequence of certain groups of koans to study out of a total of some 1,700—hence the Japanese pronunciation of names used here—but this is a purely notational arrangement. In practice, the original idea that a koan is no more than an expedient means toward entering the frame of mind of the former master to whom it is attributed has not been lost, and from this standpoint one koan is just as good as another. For what counts is not the answer but the answerer, so one

can well understand why the great Ta Hui is said to have burned his master's published koan collection for fear that students might read it simply as a training in repartee. Every educated person should be familiar with the classic koans included here, since their echoes resonate throughout subsequent East Asian Buddhism. But the original purpose of these stories was not education, not at all.

T. H. Barrett
Professor of East Asian History
School of Oriental and African Studies
University of London

THE ZEN KOAN

Zen is the traditional temple life of Buddhist Japan and Korea. Originally, the beginnings of Zen Buddhism were brought to China by the Brahmin monk Bodhidharma, a direct spiritual descendant of Buddha's disciple Mahakashyapa, around the year 520. Though Indian teachers of various forms of Buddhism had preceded him, none had been able to establish a school or a line of disciples. Centuries before Bodhidharma brought with him the *essence* of Buddha's experience—his enlightenment. Casting away the traditional paraphernalia of Buddhism, its scriptures and deities, Bodhidharma succeeded in establishing a school in China where monks practiced the seated, cross-legged meditation advocated by him, and focused their goals not upon the learning of sutras, but upon the realization of their true nature. This practice was called *dhyana*—literally meaning "meditation" in Sanskrit—which was pronounced *Ch'an* in China and, later, *Zen* in Japan, where it eventually reached its full flowering and development.

The maturing of Zen out of the flower of Buddhism, however, was a gradual process. By the Middle Ages, Buddhism had become thoroughly assimilated into Chinese life. It was an institutional presence, with temples and monasteries a common sight in cities and countryside towns, and the monks and nuns wearing their traditional costumes formed a recognizable part of the population. With the widespread acceptance of Buddhism, the basic tenets of the religion had developed into a whole new spectrum of faith and ritual among the Chinese people who venerated and worshipped Buddhism but, dangerously, were not putting into practice its original and essential message. The task of early Chinese Zen masters was thus to bring Buddhist teaching to life in the here and now, and to show that enlightenment was not a superhuman goal to be achieved over eons of time, but a state of being that could be revealed through awareness in everyday life. In order to accomplish their

role as transmitters of Buddha's original experience, Chinese masters invented a number of devices, such as koans, to give their disciples an immediate taste of Buddha's enlightenment.

What is a koan? This question must surely point us beyond the known and the unknown, to the unknowable.

Koans, literally meaning "cases," are a highly distinctive element in the history of Zen Buddhism, and there is no obvious parallel to them in the literature of any other religion. They are old Chinese-devised problems given to the Zen student for study—they are intractable, insoluble conundrums to which the disciple must find an answer. The answer, however, is not reached by any means of logic or thought; the answer is, rather, an experience, a realization. Most koans are based upon actual incidents in the lives of Zen masters and the activities of ancient monasteries. They are the answers of masters to their monks, or monks' questions to their teachers, and exchanges between enlightened masters. These are all men tremendously intent on being reborn, on satori. Their awakening through the practice of koans is one of the fundamental instruction methods of Zen. These tools, the result of spontaneous teaching, were recorded and handed down from monastery to monastery, generation to generation. Koans are used today for training students in all schools of Zen. Of the two major contemporary sects, the Rinzai places a greater emphasis upon koans, although the Soto sect uses them also.

Koans are a living memory of a time long past but still essential to our soul, when mind and logic did not rule people, but intuition and oneness with nature were the essential ways of expression and understanding. Koans are like resonating echoes of a part of ourselves that we need to call back to the surface in order to taste enlightenment. Koans are the art of turning to our own light and being illumined by it.

This book presents selections from the two major classic collections of koans—*The Gateless Gate (Mumonkan)* and *The Blue Cliff Records (Hekiganroku)*. *The Gateless Gate* is the later of the two texts, having been composed in 1228 by the Zen monk Mumon Ekai, but it is usually studied first as it is shorter and has a simpler subject. *The Blue Cliff Records* were composed by Zen master Setcho (980–1052), and the book contains illusions and paradoxes of great subtlety and difficulty. This volume is organized according to koans of ascending difficulty accompanied by brief explanations to help the reader.

The genuine insight of such Zen masters as Ummon, Hyakujo, Baso, Joshu, Obaku, and Nansen into the essence of Buddha's message was the most crucial factor to the spreading of Zen throughout China and southern Asia. They were the experts who devised and propagated conceptual systems and forms of practice, and carried on the vital work of adapting the timeless teaching to the specific needs of times and places. They were the ones who communicated the dharma at the intimate person-to-person level, seeking out people whose sincerity and capacity made them suitable candidates to carry forth the torch of Zen. Analyzed as a body of wisdom, the koan collections presented in this volume form a careful and unique study of consciousness, and of the transformation of consciousness into wisdom. This is a map, charting the inconceivable, drawn by the ones who have been there for all of us who wish to follow.

THE
GATELESS GATE

The great path has no gates,
Thousands of roads enter it.
When one passes through this gateless gate
He walks freely between heaven and earth.

CASE 7—JOSHU'S "WASH YOUR BOWL"

A monk said to Joshu, "I have just entered this monastery. Please teach me."
"Have you eaten your rice porridge?" asked Joshu. "Yes, I have,"
replied the monk. "Then you had better wash your bowl," said Joshu.
With this the monk gained enlightenment.

Joshu (778–897), who attained full realization when he was seventeen years old, was one of the greatest Chinese Zen masters. By asking whether the young monk has already eaten his breakfast, Joshu is checking the monk's level of consciousness. The first daily practice of the monks in a Zen monastery is chanting sutras on a single low note, the vibration of which penetrates the body and the mind and prepares the monks for the absolute silence (*samadhi*) of the meditation that follows. Samadhi is maintained through a breakfast of porridge that is eaten solemnly. Perceiving the hidden meaning of Joshu's apparently practical question, the monk answers, *"Yes, I have,"* meaning that he was able to maintain samadhi while eating breakfast. Joshu's answer, *"Then you had better wash your bowl,"* is the Zen way of indicating to be here and now. The monk is no longer at breakfast; he should pay attention to the present. What is past is past; wash it away with the leftovers of the porridge.

CASE 9—DAITSU CHISHO BUDDHA

A monk asked Koyo Seijo, "Daitsu Chisho Buddha sat in zazen for ten kalpas and could not attain Buddhahood. He did not become a Buddha. How could this be?" Seijo said, "Your question is quite self-explanatory." The monk asked, "He meditates so long; why could he not attain Buddhahood?" Seijo said, "Because he did not become a Buddha."

Daitsu Chisho Buddha is the Buddha of Great Penetration and Perfect Wisdom. *Kalpa* is a measure of time, hundreds of thousands of years long. It stretches between the creation and recreation of a universe. Sitting in *zazen* for ten *kalpas* is a metaphor to show that in the state of absolute samadhi there is no time. In the state of samadhi there is no enlightenment, no realization, no Buddhahood; there is just this samadhi. Therefore, Daitsu Chisho Buddha did not *become* a Buddha because he *was* a Buddha from the beginning.

CASE 15—TOZAN'S SIXTY BLOWS

Tozan came to study with Ummon. Ummon asked, "Where are you from?" "From Sato," Tozan replied. "Where were you during the summer?" "Well, I was at the monastery of Hozu, south of the lake." "When did you leave there?" Ummon asked. "On August 25," was Tozan's reply. "I spare you sixty blows," Ummon said.

The next day Tozan came to Ummon and said, "Yesterday you said you spared me sixty blows. I beg to ask you, where was I at fault?" "Oh, you rice bag!" shouted Ummon. "What makes you wander about, now west of the river, now south of the lake?" Tozan thereupon came to a mighty enlightenment experience.

Ummon (d. 949) was the founder of one of the five major schools of Zen. Tozan (910–990) was one of the four most distinguished disciples of Ummon. To spare blows to a disciple is a great insult. The disciple is not even worth the punishment of the master. When Ummon asks Tozan what good his wandering from one monastery to another is, the master is revealing that what the disciple is seeking he already possesses. He should concentrate upon bringing it to the surface, rather than wandering here, there, and everywhere. At this realization Tozan attained enlightenment.

CASE 19—NANSEN'S "ORDINARY MIND IS THE WAY"

Joshu asked Nansen, "What is the Way?" "Ordinary mind is the Way," Nansen replied. "Shall I try to seek after it?" Joshu asked. "If you try for it, you will become separated from it," responded Nansen. "How can I know the Way unless I try for it?" persisted Joshu. Nansen said, "The Way is not a matter of knowing or not knowing. Knowing is a delusion; not knowing is confusion. When you have really reached the Way beyond doubt, you will find it as vast and boundless as outer space. How can it be talked about on the level of right and wrong?" With these words, Joshu came to a sudden realization.

The ordinary Way is samadhi; it is peace of mind. When you are in samadhi, you are simply in samadhi; there is no searching after the Way. It is an experience, not a conceptual understanding. Samadhi is vast and boundless and beyond right and wrong.

CASE 21—UMMON'S "KANSHIKESTU"

A monk asked Ummon, "What is Buddha?" Ummon replied, "Kanshiketsu!"

Kanshiketsu, literally a "shit-stick," was used in old times instead of toilet paper. Shit-sticks become dirty to clean us. If this is not a Buddha, then what is? Out of gratitude to the stick, we call them Buddhas.

CASE 29—THE SIXTH PATRIARCH'S "YOUR MIND MOVES"

Two monks were arguing about a flag. One said, "The flag is moving."
The other said, "The wind is moving."
The sixth patriarch happened to be passing by. He told them,
"Not the wind, not the flag; mind is moving."

It used to be the custom of Zen temples that when a master was delivering a sermon, a flag was hoisted at the gate to announce it to the public. Two monks became distracted by the flag and started an argument. The sixth patriarch's remark led them to introspect into the nature of their minds.

CASE 32—A NON-BUDDHIST PHILOSOPHER QUESTIONS THE BUDDHA

A philosopher asked Buddha,
"Without words, without the wordless, will you tell me truth?"
The Buddha kept silence.
The philosopher bowed and thanked the Buddha, saying, "With your
loving kindness I have cleared away my delusions and entered the true path."
After the philosopher had gone, Ananda asked the Buddha what the philosopher
had attained.
The Buddha replied, "A good horse runs even at the shadow of the whip."

Buddha's silence—his samadhi—was the subtle lesson that the master taught to the philosopher. The subtlety of the teaching is like the shadow; the impact of enlightenment is the whip.

CASE 38—A BUFFALO PASSES BY THE WINDOW

Goso said, "A buffalo passes by the window. His head, horns, and four legs all go past. But why can't the tail pass too?"

"A buffalo passes by the window" is a metaphor for what happens during the practice of *zazen*. Thoughts, emotions, sensations all pass through consciousness as though they were clouds traveling across a clear sky. The head, the horns, and the four legs all go past: the activity of consciousness dies away when one enters samadhi during *zazen*. The tail, a metaphor for samadhi, can't pass because samadhi itself never passes away.

CASE 40—TIPPING OVER A VASE

Hyakujo wished to send a monk to open a new monastery. He told his disciples that whoever answered a question most ably would be appointed. Placing a water vase on the ground, he asked, "Who can say what this is without calling its name?" The chief monk said, "No one can call it a wooden shoe." Isan, the cooking monk, tipped over the vase with his foot and went out. Hyakujo smiled and said, "The chief monk loses." And Isan became the master of the new monastery.

The truth, here symbolized by the water vase, cannot either be told nor not be told; it can only be shown. Isan, a monk who studied with Hyakujo for twenty years, made a striking demonstration of this teaching.

CASE 41—BODHIDHARMA'S MIND-PACIFYING

Bodhidharma sat facing the wall. The second patriarch stood in the snow. He cut off his arm and presented it to Bodhidharma, crying, "My mind has no peace as yet! I beg you, master, please pacify my mind!" "Bring your mind here and I will pacify it for you," replied Bodhidharma. "I have searched for my mind, and I cannot take hold of it," said the second patriarch. "Now your mind is pacified," said Bodhidharma.

Bodhidharma came from India to China around the year 520 and eventually settled in the kingdom of Wei where he practiced his "wall-gazing meditation" for nine years. The second patriarch, Bodhidharma's first disciple, was Eka. Legend tells that Eka wanted so badly to be taught by Bodhidharma that he cut his arm off in order to attract the attention of the master who was deep in samadhi. At this extreme gesture, Bodhidharma consented to help Eka pacify his mind by asking him to bring it to him. How can mind be brought anywhere? Eka, confronted with this request by the master, finds that he cannot get hold of his mind, much less bring it forth. The realization of no-mind brings immediate peace; the search for mind is frustrating until we realize that the search and the goal are one path leading to emptiness.

CASE 46—PROCEED ON FROM THE TOP OF THE POLE

Sekiso Osho asked, "How can you proceed on further from the top of a hundred-foot pole?" Another eminent teacher of old said, "You, who sit on top of a hundred-foot pole, although you have entered the Way you are not yet genuine. Proceed on from the top of the pole, and you will show your whole body in the ten directions."

Sekiso Soen (986–1039) is here addressed as Sekiso Osho, the latter being a term of honor used for Zen masters. To be on top of a hundred-foot pole is a metaphor to indicate that Sekiso had attained a high level of consciousness, but he could not see how to proceed further. In the practice of meditation, one may come to a sort of extremity, to the brink at the edge of an abyss, where death is faced. This is a crucial moment in which a disciple might become panic-stricken. The elder master gives valuable advice to Sekiso; by hinting that he is not genuine, he indicates that, although Sekiso has attained a high level of consciousness, this condition is still measurable, bound, and not completely free from all attachments. The master wants Sekiso to go beyond the attachment to Buddhahood and samadhi. By proceeding on further from the pole, Sekiso will leave behind his attachments and attain complete freedom. *"You will show your body in the ten directions"* means freedom.

THE BLUE CLIFF RECORDS

Smoke over the hill indicates fire, horns over the fence indicate an ox. Given one corner, you grasp the other three; one glance, and you discern the smallest difference. Such quickness, however, is only too common among robed monks. When you have stopped the deluded activity of consciousness, then, whatever situation you may find yourself in, you enjoy perfect freedom, in adversity and prosperity, in taking and giving. Now tell me, how in fact will this sort of person behave? See Setcho's complications.

CASE 3—BASO'S "SUN-FACED BUDDHA, MOON-FACED BUDDHA"

The great master Baso was seriously ill. The chief priest of the temple came to pay his respects. He asked, "How do you feel these days?" The master said, "Sun-faced Buddha, Moon-faced Buddha."

Baso (709–88) was a peak in ancient Zen history. A total of 139 eminent Zen teachers had been his disciples. Baso's words "Sun-faced Buddha, Moon-faced Buddha" became one of the most famous sayings in Zen. Imagine being in the glorious presence of the setting sun at the far end of an ocean. Moment by moment the golden-faced Buddha sinks below the horizon, while, on the other side over the mountains, the moon is rising, inclined a little in her musing. It is in moments like these that everything is silent; the glory and the radiance bring us into absolute samadhi.

CASE 6—UMMON'S "EVERY DAY IS A GOOD DAY"

Ummon addressed the assembly and said, "I am not asking you about the days
before the fifteenth of the month. But what about after the fifteenth?
Come and give me a word about those days."
And he himself gave the answer for them: "Every day is a good day."

The days before the fifteenth of the month could be the days before today, or
the days before you were born, or the days before your enlightenment.
Ummon is not asking about what has happened before the present moment.
"What happens after the fifteenth?" is Ummon's way of asking what happens to
consciousness at this point in time and in the future. No one could answer
Ummon, so he gave the answer himself—when you are in samadhi, every day
is a good day, you don't ask about the past, nor wonder about the future. You
are here, you are now.

CASE 9—JOSHU'S "FOUR GATES"

A monk asked Joshu, "What is Joshu?"
Joshu said, "The East Gate, the West Gate, the North Gate, the South Gate."

Master Joshu came from a town also called Joshu, which was walled and had four gates, one in each corner. Joshu, the master, also has four gates—conversion to Zen Buddhism, training in *zazen* and koans, enlightenment in everyday activity, and the attainment of final nirvana. Joshu is indicating that anyone can pass his own gates and come for instruction. But unless a disciple has made progress through his training he cannot pass the gates; it is not Joshu who is blocking you, but you yourself.

CASE 11—OBAKU'S "PARTAKERS OF BREWER'S GRAIN"

*Obaku addressed the assembly and said, "You are all partakers of brewer's grain.
If you go on studying Zen like that, you will never finish it. Do you know that in
the land of T'ang there is no Zen teacher?"*

*Then a monk came forward and said, "But surely there are those who teach disciples
and preside over the assemblies. What about that?"*

Obaku said, "I do not say that there is no Zen, but that there is no Zen teacher."

Obaku (d. 850) succeeded Hyakujo and was the teacher of Rinzai, founder of
the Rinzai line of Zen. To be a partaker of brewer's grain has become a popu-
lar saying used to belittle all those who imitate Zen masters of old times. The
meaning of these words is that you eat the grain left over by the brewers after
they have made beer and then think that you are having a taste of the real
thing. In stating that there is no Zen teacher, Obaku is reaffirming one of the
strongest lessons in Zen—it cannot be taught. You must attain it by your own
practice, study, and research.

CASE 14—UMMON'S "PREACHING FACING ONENESS"

A monk asked Ummon, "What is the teaching of the Buddha's lifetime?"
Ummon said, "Preaching facing oneness."

Zen masters deliver their sermons facing the image of the Buddha. However, the meaning of this koan is broader: oneness is absolute truth. To face oneness means to face every thing—yourself, the world, every being, and every thing—in its absolute truth.

LIST OF COLOUR PLATES

ACKNOWLEDGMENTS

The editors gratefully acknowledge the following sources:

Zen Flesh, Zen Bones, Paul Reps, Charles E. Tuttle Co. Inc. of Tokyo, Japan

Two Zen Classics-The Gateless Gate and The Blue Cliff Records, Katsuki Sekida, trans., Weatherhill, New York

BIBLIOGRAPHY

Reps, Paul. *Zen Flesh, Zen Bones*. Rutland and Tokyo: Charles E. Tuttle Co., 1957.

Sekida, Katsuki, trans. *Two Zen Classics-The Gateless Gate and the Blue Cliff Records*. New York: Weatherhill, 1995.

Holstein, Alexander. *Pointing at the Moon.*
Rutland and Tokyo: Charles E. Tuttle Co., 1993.

Osho. *No Water, No Moon.* Poona, India: Osho
Foundation International, 1972.

——. *Zen: The Path of Paradox.* Vols. 1–3.
Poona, India: Osho Foundation International, 1973.

——. *Zen: The Special Transmission.*
Poona, India: Osho Foundation International, 1974.

Reps, Paul. *Zen Flesh, Zen Bones.*
Rutland and Tokyo: Charles E. Tuttle Co., 1957.

Sasaki, Ruth Fuller, Yoshitaka Iriya, and Dana Fraser, trans.
A Man of Zen—The Recorded Sayings of Layman P'ang.
New York: Weatherhill, 1992.

Sekida, Katsuki, trans. *Two Zen Classics—The Gateless Gate and
The Blue Cliff Records.* New York: Weatherhill, 1995.

Manuela Dunn Mascetti is the author of *The Song of Eve, Saints, Goddess*, and coauthor with Peter Lorie of *The Quotable Spirit*. A Zen student of many years, she lives in London with her husband and her two Tiffanies named after Zen monks.

Professor Timothy Hugh Barrett, formerly Head of the History Department at the prestigious London School of Oriental and African Studies, is an expert on East Asian History who has studied Zen in both Japan and China for many years.